I Am the Violet Tara
Goddess of Forgiveness and Freedom

———

Peter Mt. Shasta

Published by Church of the Seven Rays
Post Office Box 711
Mount Shasta, California 96067
www.I-AM-Teachings.com

Copyright 2019 by Peter Mt. Shasta

ISBN: 9780998414393

No part of this book may be reproduced, stored in a retrieval system, or transmitted by any means without the written permission of the author. Request for such permission should be addressed to the publisher.

Other books by Peter Mt. Shasta:

"I AM" the Open Door

"I AM" Affirmations and the Secret of their Effective Use

"I AM" The Living Christ

Search for the Guru:
Adventures of a Western Mystic, Book I

Apprentice to the Masters:
Adventures of a Western Mystic: Book II

My Search in Tibet for the Secret Wish-Fulfilling Jewel

Lady Master Pearl, My Teacher

Step By Step, Ascended Master Discourses

It is What it Is: Further Adventures of a Western Mystic

Note of Thanks

I would like to thank William J. Barnett, Caitlin Bean, Yemana Sanders and Rebecca Burns Tufano, who provided invaluable assistance editing the text; also, Susanne Meyer, who helped with the graphics.

***

Don't mistake mere words to be the meaning of the teachings. Mingle the practice with your own being and attain liberation from samsara right now.

-Padmasambhava

Table of Contents

Dedication 7

Preface 9

Foreword 15

Prologue 21

Goddess Tara 25

Invocation 29

Dedication of Merit 31

Basic Practices 33

Taking Refuge 35

Foundation Practices 37

Developing Compassion 45

Basic Goodness 49

Forgiveness 51

Still the Mind with Six Nails 55

Invoking God 57

"I Am" is the Key 61

The Preliminaries 63

Prayer to the I AM Presence: 67

Archangel Michael 73

Kama Tantra 75

Invocation of the Violet Tara 79

Request for Empowerment 83

Becoming the Tara 85

Dissolution 87

Gratitude 89

Note 91

The Nature of Mind 93

Dedication

This book is dedicated to Carl Goldsmith, my great grandfather, who in approximately 1865 was the first known American to visit Tibet. The stories of his adventures in the Far East told to me as a child by my grandmother, Hannah Anhalt, sparked my first interest in visiting the "land of snows." When in 1994, I finally walked under the arch of the stone gate near the Potala Palace in Lhasa, this dream to seek the ancient wisdom of Tibet was realized.

Preface

As luminous beings, we sacrificed some of that luminosity with our decision to eat of the fruit from the tree of knowledge of good and evil. To learn this lesson and acquire the wisdom and compassion we sought, we entered into animal bodies who had to struggle for survival. Thus arose the need to preserve these bodies, and hence the generation of ego. Fully identified with the dense body and its needs, the ego asserted almost full control. In fact, we forgot who we truly are and began to identify with the ego.

The egoic mind organizes reality according to boundaries: good and evil, mine and yours, pleasure and pain, right and wrong, good and bad. Ego sets itself as the master of the mind, programming it according to its needs. However, this life in duality does not lead to happiness. We find ourselves banished from the Garden of Eden into the mundane world—the *samsara* of struggle in the world of constantly changing dreams. People think *I will be happy when I get everything I want,* but that moment never arrives.

Occasionally a brave soul made a quest into the mountains or the depths of the forest to find the secret of happiness. Occasionally one succeeded and emerged with clues to share, and over time specific teachings emerged. Some of these teachings have been codified into religions, which eventually lost most of the original essence and became tools to control people's minds instead of liberate them. It is my intent to share here some of the ancient teachings that will help you remember who you truly are.

To remember who you are you must understand the egoic mind. It is similar to a computer operating system bundled with various pre-installed applications, one of which operates as the ego. The ego controls many sub-programs such as emotions, thoughts, and beliefs, that activate automatically in various situations as fear, anger, violence, jealousy, attachment, desire, aversion, pride, vanity, and laziness—all of which are the result of ignorance.[1]

The first step to remembering who you are is to know that the mind, emotions, sensations and the body are not you—the real you is beyond all these. They are only functions of your operating system. Why not login as the Administrator and delete those aspects of your mind that have been holding you back from operating at your full capacity, and from attaining freedom. To find out who you really are, you need to break your identification with that operating system and assert your full dominion as the Administrator. That step cannot occur while the ego programs are loaded and operating. If you try to edit the

---

[1] Buddhists lump these together as the Five Poisons that we transform into the Five Wisdoms, while the Bible talks about the Seven Deadly Sins as opposed to the Seven Virtues.

code, then the system will crash, and you will become non-functional. However, if you shut down the ego for a while and go for a walk in the forest, sit and meditate, you will find there is a vaster world, a larger program. You will find the larger mind—consciousness itself, which lies beyond the control of the human self.

The mind runs all sensory and mental data through algorithms to maintain the illusion that the computer is in control. It does not compute vagueness, uncertainty, or multiple possible answers. There is only one right answer, one right way to do everything, and it does not like to be wrong.

Mysticism is a completely foreign element to the ego because it does not fit any algorithm, nor does it appear to foster material survival, be of benefit to the body, or increase one's material status. Hence, the mind tries to prevent any attempt at reprogramming. Your screen may go blank, and then you need to press the reset button. That is what this book offers, a way to reset your mind.

Resetting the mind requires bold action. There are several ways to achieve a "reset," some of them spontaneous, but they can prove to be traumatic and are often dangerous:

1) Near-death experiences: Your body dies, and you experience conscious existence beyond the body, ego, personality, and conventional mind.

Then your body revives and your system reboots with a larger and more intuitive operating system, assuming you recover fully.

2) Emotional shock: Someone dies unexpectedly, your partner leaves you, your home is destroyed in an earthquake or war, you are fired and become homeless. The uncertainty caused by this shock forces the mind to let go of its routine program and search for a more inclusive view of reality.

3) Grace: You have a sudden insight independent of anything. This can sometimes be given by a Master or your Higher Self, independent of any external happening. These insights can come at any moment and without preparation. The Zen tradition calls these *kensho* experiences.

4) Entheogens: Throughout history people close to nature have used plant substances to transcend the boundaries of the rational mind. Many of these substances supply DMT, the same molecule produced by the human pineal gland. These substances, such as certain mushrooms and ayahuasca, should be taken only when there is direct inner guidance, and when there

are no mental or physical contraindications.

5) Meditation: You still your mind and inquire into the nature of the self. Other forms of meditation are light and sound meditation, also *Vajrayana,* which uses visualization, mantra, and mudra (rituals or hand gestures) to deconstruct the mundane mind. There is also Zen, and Dzogchen, where the mind is observed in the moment and without the support of any concrete practice.

No matter what it takes to awaken you, if you survive the experience you will need to assimilate your new awareness into your human life. It is toward that end that the practices here are offered.

Foreword

This inspiration for this book was given as an instantaneous transmission by the Ascended Master Saint Germain.[2] He did not channel the text, as he wanted me to express the teachings in my own words, which will be easier for others treading the same path as myself to understand. The process of bringing forth these teachings has also been more conducive to my own growth than if he had dictated them. As he has often said, "The age for channeling is over. You need to find the truth within yourself." He did, however, watch over my shoulder and impress on me the ideas he wished to bring forth.

Although the teachings given here have existed in various cultures in the past, Saint Germain began releasing the fundamentals to Western humanity through Guy Ballard (Godfrey Ray King) in the 1930s. The primary teachings he gave at that time were:

---

[2] Saint Germain is the Ascended Master Chohan (head) of the 7th Ray, also known as the Violet Ray. He is the Member of the Ascended Council of Light (Great White Brotherhood) that has been specifically working for the freedom and liberation of Western civilization for the past few centuries. He dwells in the etheric realms yet manifests as a physical presence as needed.

1) God is your own Higher Self.[3]

2) That Self is called into action by the words, "I Am." Whatever follows those words comes into manifestation.

3) By purifying your *karma*, negative consequences of past actions, you can ascend and merge with your Higher Self.[4]

4) You can purify yourself with an aspect of consciousness known as the Violet Consuming Flame.

Further teachings were introduced at the request of Saint Germain in my book, *Search in Tibet for the Secret Wish-Fulfilling Jewel* (Church of the Seven Rays, 2016). These *tantric* teachings on the invocation of the Violet Tara introduce advanced elements to purify the mind in

---

[3] The three bodies of the self that are described in Buddhism are the Nirmanakaya (personal self), Sambogakaya (higher mental body or soul), and the Dharmakaya (I AM Presence or *atman* in Sanskrit)

[4] Ascension is a process well known in Tibet as *jalus*.

order to attain liberation.[5] Although enlightenment can be attained by other methods—even spontaneously—these methods provided here outline a progression of steps that can be consciously pursued and that have proven over the centuries to yield dependable results.

The chief problem I have had in presenting these teachings in contemporary language is that the present age is quite different from India and Tibet in the ninth century, when many of these teachings were first put into written form. No longer are there enlightened siddhas, lamas, or gurus easily available to bestow empowerments, give teachings, and answer questions when needed. In one sense this is a blessing, for it forces you to go inward and contact the Inner Guru, the I AM Presence, which is always there and waiting for you. You can also connect directly with the Ascended Masters, whom I call here the Ascended Council of Light (formerly referred to as the Great White Brotherhood) and petition them personally rather than having to rely on a lama or guru who is fallible and often not available when you need them. The Ascended Masters are always available. The key, however, is learning how to recognize their response, as

---

[5] *Tantra* (Sanskrit: unbroken thread of awareness) is another term for *Vajrayana* (Sanskrit: thunderbolt awareness vehicle). This is the third vehicle of Buddhism, the first two being, *Theravada* (later called *Hinayana)*, relying on written precepts to attain personal liberation, and *Mahayana* (the path of the *Bodhisattva)*, the dedication to achieve enlightenment for the benefit of all sentient beings, rather than just oneself.

well as that of your Higher Self, which often comes as a simple prompting of the heart—often called *the still small voice*. Be assured, whether you perceive it or not, everyone is under the guidance of at least one of these great beings. All humanity lives within their ashrams and are watched over by them as a parent watches over their child.

In place of many Sanskrit terms such as *lama, yiddam, and dakini*, which are intrinsic parts of tantric yoga, I have used more common Western terms. Out of these three components, I have continued to use only *yidam* (meditational Deity), as there is no precise Western equivalent. This is a Deity we create out of our own consciousness in the manner of a thought form. How real this Deity becomes is up to us.

The terms for the Three Jewels, *Buddha, Dharma, and Sangha,* have also been translated into modern spiritual terms. The image of the Buddha sitting in meditation is a placeholder image representing an awakened being, not the historical Shakyamuni Buddha, who is now an Ascended Master. Thus, I have substituted the Ascended Master, who is present and can hear your prayers, and who represents an ideal to which you can aspire.

The terms *dakini* and *daka* (Sanskrit: sky dancer) are more difficult to replace, as they represent not only Ascended Masters, but all who transmit wisdom and enlightenment, including human teachers, and occasionally a friend, partner, or even a stranger.

Lastly, in place of Vajrasattva, the yiddam Tibetans visualize as the source of all the Gods, I have substituted the I AM Presence. Since it is the I AM Consciousness that creates everything anyway, rather than visualize an intermediary Deity, why not visualize that I AM Presence? We then invoke the Violet Tara directly—out of ourselves.

Of course, since she is a manifestation of the Divine Mother who is everywhere, she can arise spontaneously. The point of this practice is that since everything you perceive is created and qualified by your own mind, by consciously invoking the Violet Tara into action, you begin to manifest her qualities of forgiveness and compassion—and achieve your own self-mastery and freedom. This type of visualization is a key element of the Tibetan Buddhist practice.

Prologue

Out of the sea of consciousness emerge the awareness of love and thought—different aspects of the One. Similarly, the sun's light and heat are perceived as different, though from the same Source. From this joyous birth of dual consciousness comes forth the sound: Om—the primordial sound—followed by the vibrations now known as the Sanskrit alphabet.[6] Then emanated the seven rays of consciousness which, as they enter the density of the atmosphere, sometimes appear as the seven colors of the rainbow. One manifests as many. Consciousness manifests as sound, light, and the colors: red, orange, yellow, green, blue, violet, and indigo. It also manifests in the denser expressions of the elements: earth, water, air, fire, and ether; and out of these components came forth all that is.

From this Mother-Father God consciousness were born the children of God, like rays of the sun, radiating to all parts of Creation. These Suns of God, endowed by the Creator with self-will, began to express that will wherever they went, creating and experimenting on their own. Those who entered animal bodies became known as humanity. This race that had never known duality, had the desire to know the nature of good and evil. The beings of light who remained in the higher worlds we call angels (Greek: messengers), or *devas* (Sanskrit: shining ones).

---

[6] In all countries of the world, infants make the same initial sounds regardless of native language, sounds that are the basis for the vowels and consonants of Sanskrit: Ah, Ee, Oo, Um, Ma, Pa, Da, Ka, etc.

Once the understanding of the nature of good and evil is learned, and the consequent wisdom and compassion is realized, then we can "eat of the tree of eternal life" and ascend again as beings of light—and become an Ascended Master. This process of ascension is known in Tibet as the attainment of the Rainbow Body (Tibetan, *jalus*). The Christian Bible refers to the ascension of several beings, among them Enoch and Jesus:

> ***Enoch walked with God, and he was not; for God took him.***
>
> -Genesis 5:24
>
> ***While they beheld, he was taken up; and a cloud received him out of their sight.***
>
> -Acts 1:9

This raising process is available to all—taking place to some degree every time our attention is turned inward to the Source. Only the preoccupation with your thoughts and emotions keeps you from realizing your enlightenment. What your attention is on, you become, so if your attention is on anger, you become angry. This dynamic is controlled by your ego, which dictates your perceptions and delusions. However, if your attention is on the Light, you become the Light; on Love you become Love. Every morning before you awaken, you are in a state of emptiness, of no-thought, but as your habitual personality returns, you are back in the ever changing, illusory world of *samsara*. Thus, only through stilling the mind do you awaken from the dream of your personality and realize you are not that. Your True Self is beyond all thoughts, sensations, and concepts—and is eternally happy.

To arrive at that emptiness, you must deconstruct the matrix—the illusion you call your "self." This deconstruction is accomplished in meditation—by realizing that your life is a dream you can change. You can deconstruct and reconstruct this dream as you wish. In this way you penetrate the heart of reality and achieve Mastery in that reality. Mastery is not achieved by accumulating more information, by listening to channeled messages, or sitting at the feet of a guru. Self-Mastery is a simple concept yet requires application at every moment. Every thought and feeling must be observed. You simply have to take your mind apart and put it back together, and no one can do that but you. The practice given here, calling forth the Violet Tara—realizing your oneness with Her—manifesting Her Activity—and finally reappearing as a regenerated self—will help you attain Mastery. It will also release the activity of the Violet Consuming Flame to purify humanity.

As you slow the incessant flow of thoughts, you begin to experience the gap between thoughts, and you learn to dwell in that gap. In that space you rest in timeless awareness and experience your basic goodness. You also find within your oneness with others—regardless of appearances—because all originate from the same Source. We are all children of the same God, characters in the same dream—and all those characters in the dream are images of yourself—endowed with basic goodness.

In meditation the question arises,

Who am I?

You can only find the answer to that question by examining,

Who is it that wants to know?

In this process of self-inquiry, you find the observer that is beyond all thought, emotion, and action. You have the choice at every moment to identify with the personality that reacts to stimuli or the impersonal self who observes the stimuli. While watching an exciting film, you may forget you are only an observer and react as though you were a character in the film—but you are only an observer in a theater, perceiving images of light on a screen. In the same way you can see life as a film—and you don't need to react.

Who are you? What role are you playing? Why? Can you change the next scene? Who is the script writer of your life, the producer, and director? Who are the other actors? Is there even an "other?" Answering these questions, you awaken to your True Self. You begin to play the lead role in your movie more consciously. As you awaken, you help others awaken.

Goddess Tara

Tara has been regarded as the feminine aspect of God—the Divine Mother—for thousands of years throughout Asia. As the mother, she observes and feels compassion for all her children. In her form of the Violet Tara, she dissolves negative energy, transmutes the karmic consequences of past actions, and helps people feel forgiveness of others. Like Saint Germain—the Ascended Master who directs the Violet Ray for the Earth—she clears emotional obstacles to freedom.

Tara means "star" in Sanskrit but is also the verb "to cross over." As the North Star she helps sailors navigate at night, so in a sense she helps us cross over the sea of illusion known as *samsara.* Another translation is "pupil of the eye," so she is one who has the all-seeing eye keeping watch constantly over her children. She not only liberates us from the delusion of duality but dissolves all negative energy and raises us into a higher frequency. She is omnipresent and spontaneously arising—a part of our own consciousness—waiting to be called forth at any moment.

All cultures, except the present Judeo Christian one, recognize the dual aspect of Creation, that all is composed of female and male aspects; hence, they have recognized and honored the Divine Mother—a compassionate being who helps her children in whatever way she can. She is an ally of women, establishing respect for the feminine principle and creating equal opportunities for women everywhere. The Tibetan culture believes she emanates twenty-one different forms, white, green, red, and so forth, each having specific functions, and practices, although no colors are specified beyond white, red, and green. This is the first time the Goddess has been revealed in her aspect as the Violet Tara.

Tibetan literature reports that Tara was born on a distant planet and was confronted by a monk who said, "It's too bad you are a woman, as you will not be able to achieve liberation in that form." She replied, "I vow to not only achieve liberation as a woman, but to incarnate in female form in all future lifetimes on all planets until samsara is emptied."

In a subsequent lifetime she incarnated on Earth and on encountering Shariputra, one of the foremost disciples of Shakyamuni Buddha, was astounded to hear him express a similar limited view of women. After listening patiently, she used her extraordinary power to transform him into a woman. Then she changed herself into a man that resembled Shariputra. "So, how does it feel to be a woman?" Tara asked with amusement, "Is consciousness the same or different?"

"Consciousness is the same in both forms," he replied, amazed. She then transformed them both back into their original forms and said, in parting,

I will continue to manifest as a woman until all beings realize, as you just have, that consciousness transcends form.

With that exclamation, she disappeared. She now appears wherever needed to those whose minds are open.

Invocation

Beloved Goddess Tara,
Mother of the Violet Flame of Forgiveness,
Help us overcome the illusions
Of the world.
Free us from ignorance and
Help us achieve enlightenment.
Grant us the ability to forgive and
Feel compassion for others.
Clear all negative energy and
Raise our consciousness.
We pray to you, come to us now,
Violet Tara—Mother of the Violet Fire.

Dedication of Merit

Merit should not be thought of as an award, but as energy acquired through spiritual practice. A leap in evolution occurs when you dedicate that energy for the benefit of others.

> Throughout my many lives until this very moment, whatever virtue I have accomplished, including the merit generated by this practice, and all that I will ever attain, this I offer for the welfare of sentient beings.

> May sickness, war, famine, and suffering
> Be decreased for every being, while their wisdom and compassion increase in this and every future lifetime.

> May I clearly perceive all experiences to be as insubstantial as the dream fabric of the night, and instantly awaken to perceive the pure wisdom display

in the arising of every phenomenon.
May I quickly attain enlightenment in
order to work ceaselessly for the liberation
of all sentient beings.
So be it!

Basic Practices

The most basic of all spiritual practices is to contemplate the **Four Noble Truths:**

1) **Do not expect lasting happiness** on earth, as everything in duality is impermanent.
2) Suffering is caused by **attachment to desires.**
3) There is **a way** to avoid suffering.
4) The **Eight-Fold Path to Happiness** comes from practicing the correct view, intention, speech, action, livelihood, effort, mindfulness, and meditation. The foundation for achieving freedom and happiness is through living ethically and honorably according to these basic precepts. Even advanced practitioners must live according to these principles.

Taking Refuge

To begin on the path of awakening, you make a formal commitment known as Taking Refuge. Traditionally, this is made to a Lama or other authorized teacher; however, this commitment can also be made on the inner planes to one of the Ascended Masters. Refuge does not mean hiding but making a commitment to dedicate your life to awakening. To follow this path commit yourself to the:

1) **Buddha:** Awakening to your True Self.
2) **Dharma:** Practice the teachings that lead to awakening.
3) **Sangha:** Participate with the Ascended Masters as well as fellow practitioners on the path.

Foundation Practices

To still the mind, the most basic practice is *shamatha* (Pali: calm-abiding). This is followed by and combined with *vipassana* (Pali: insight, realization).[7] Only after establishing and stabilizing the process of stilling the mind and inquiring into one's true nature, should you embark on tantric meditation *(Vajrayana)*. Without establishing basic mindfulness, you can become lost in a dream of Gods and Goddesses without ever awakening to who you are. Once self-awareness is established you can see the Deities as aspects of yourself.

As you progress in your awakening, you see your dream is made of components (Sanskrit: *skandhas,* aggregates) that influence how things appear to you. You realize you are perceiving your life through the filter of thoughts, feelings, emotions, and the five senses—perceptions which may not bare any semblance to external truth. Yet, exposed to these various stimuli, and according to how you have been programmed by past experience, you react.

These aggregates of awareness are like pre-installed software applications in the computer of your mind, applications that have been programmed by past experience and that are triggered by present false data. These applications need to either be reprogrammed or deleted entirely.

---

[7] I have given more detailed instructions for these practices in *"I AM Affirmations and the Secret of Their Effective Use.* Live instruction is given in most centers of Shambhala.org.

For example, if in a past life you were a sailor and died in a shipwreck, you may have an aversion to the ocean; but instead, if you lived in a desert, the ocean may seem a paradise. The ocean itself is neither good nor bad, pleasant nor unpleasant; your perception of the ocean is simply based on your past experience. Each person is made up of these pre-programmed attractions, aversions, and concepts. Instead of deluding yourself into thinking you are the only one who knows the truth, you can observe these mental filters in action—like clouds passing across the face of the sun—and rest in non-reactive and non-conceptual awareness.

By way of further example, imagine you walk down a path in the forest and suddenly see a snake coiled to strike. You are afraid and jump out. You wonder, *is it following me?* You look back. It is still there, coiled, motionless, waiting to strike you. *Is it poisonous?*—Now you see it is not a snake, but a piece of rope! Though the snake was not real, it caused a real reaction. Your belief caused you fear, so much so that your heart raced. You could have had a heart attack and died because of your belief!

You must therefore examine your perceptions to see which are real and which are illusions, knowing ultimately that all perceptions are merely components of your dream. Then you become master of your own mind. You choose which images you want to have as a reality in your life. This practice of self-inquiry is preliminary to practicing *tantra*.[8]

Tantra enables you to have power to be who you want to be within the dream. What do you want? You can be a victim and gain sympathy from others for as long as you want; or perhaps you would rather be CEO of a corporation whose self-worth is determined by sales figures; or you could be compassionate and help others—choose your dream! Every morning as you awaken you make the same habitual choices that make you the same self, although you could change that. If you want to change, then let go of those mental habits. Look at the components that make up your mind and personality and dissolve those things you don't want and recreate yourself as a Master.

Every day we are beset by stimuli that trigger the same survival reactions as the delusion of the snake. Perhaps it's a news story that makes you angry, yet another person with different applications installed, differently programmed aggregates, feels happy over that news. Later you find the story was wrong—false news—now you are happy and the other person angry, not because of reality, but because of a pre-programmed perception. So, control your mind to control your reality. How you react to stimuli is up to you. Do you wish to constantly be manipulated by external events? Or would you rather

---

[8] *Tantra* (Sanskrit: continuity, unbroken web), seeing that everything is an aspect of ourselves, we can use everything to work on ourselves and awaken in consciousness.

control your own destiny? To change your destiny, simply look at yourself.

Look at yourself in this present moment and ask,

What am I feeling?

Describe your feelings to yourself. At first your description may take a few minutes to describe. Now, reduce your description to three words: "I feel..." (Try not to say "I am feeling" for using "I Am" amplifies whatever follows those words). For example, you can say, "I was walking along a path in the forest and saw a snake and panicked, but the snake turned out to only be a rope; however, I thought I was going to die and panicked." Then, reduce that description to simply "I felt fear," then simply, "fear." As you do this observe your in-breath and out-breath over and over. As you became calm, continue observing your emotions until the emotion subsides. Then affirm,

I am being shown what I can learn

from this experience.

Or you can ask yourself,

I created this situation to learn...?

Complete the sentence and see what thoughts, words and feelings arise. Don't analyze—just see what naturally arises to the forefront of awareness. For example, the realization from the encounter with the illusory snake could be:

> **I created this experience to see how easily**
> **I'm affected by illusions**
> **that have no basis.**

Look at the fear you felt. See it as a mechanism, neither good nor bad, that simply wanted to protect your body and prolong life. Then ask,

> **What else threatens me?**
> **When do I feel threatened,**
> **And how do I react?**
> **Is this reaction based on knowledge**
> **of the absolute truth of the situation?**

You might wonder: *Is my partner attracted to someone else? Is my boss going to fire me? Is the economy going to crash? Is the world about to end?* Your body-mind works on perceptions, not certainties, and the perceptions are most often partially wrong—often completely wrong. Remember the rope you perceived to be a snake. Instead of holding on to the trauma, you could have released it with thoughts such as,

> **It was not my time to die.**

Even if my body died,

I would still be alive.

I am grateful for being reminded

of the preciousness of life.

I see how easily I can be mistaken.

I will use every moment to see through my

illusions about people I fear,

so I see their True Nature and

feel compassion for them.

Now, come back to the present moment. Observe your in-breath and out-breath. Feel the tranquility as your thoughts slow and your attention comes to rest in the space between thoughts. Experience the tranquility of basic awareness, free of thought. Observe yourself.

Some situations are more complicated than the snake, especially relationships; but the resolution is the same. Describe the situation. What do you feel? Reduce the description to one sentence, "When the other person does this, I feel…." Reduce it further to its most basic raw emotion, such as: anger, fear, hurt, lonely, confused, rejected, judged, insulted, abandoned, and so on…. Sit with it as an image you observe separate from you, as though watching a movie in which you and the other person are characters, and you wonder, "What is the purpose of this scene? What did the Director have in mind here? However, you are the Director! At any moment you can yell "Cut! We're going to do the scene over, but differently…over and over until we get it right."

Your emotions are dark clouds passing across the face of the sun. If the emotion is strong, focus more on observing the breath until you can handle it. Realize,

This is a dream from which

I am now waking!

As you rest longer and longer in the peace between the surges of emotion, go back to the statement, "I feel…." This self-inquiry invokes your internal therapist—the Inner Guru. As you go back and forth from the empty awareness to the thoughts and emotions, the charge of the incident will fade away.

See the situations in which you react habitually—and how you can reprogram your automatic response. As you rest more and more in the stillness, this tranquility will carry over into daily life. Next time the same situation occurs your reaction will be less, until finally you don't react at all. You may realize that, beyond changing your reactions, you need to take specific action, such as: to communicate your feelings, to express a desire to change the dynamics, or even to end the relationship. This means you do not use your quest for enlightenment to bypass real life emotion, for it is precisely in dealing with these situations that we find true freedom and self-mastery.

Remember, the personalities are not real. They are simply temporary response mechanisms operating on partial data—software with glitches, programmable components that can be altered or even completely erased.

Only in the dream do they appear real. Use the methods to awaken from the dream. Free yourself from the matrix! You are the Creator, constantly reanimating your part of the matrix with your every thought. Observe, and go beyond. You are a caterpillar discovering you have become your True Self...a butterfly!

Developing Compassion

The core of all spiritual practice is the development of compassion (Latin: *com* with, *pati,* to suffer), meaning "to suffer with." Christianity calls it Charity, a word that originally meant expressing Love rather than giving handouts. Buddhism calls it *bodhicitta,* the desire for all beings to be free of suffering. The Tibetan core practice to develop compassion is giving and taking (Tibetan: *tonglen*), experiencing other's suffering in your heart and giving back love. Before you begin advanced practices, tonglen is used to generate the right motivation. Without right motivation you might find that you cherish your ego more than others or begin feeling superior to others rather than loving them. Some beginners start feeling they are superior to others now that they are doing advanced practices. To avoid this self-cherishing, prostrations and tonglen are practiced. It is also why we dedicate the merit of our practice for the benefit of others.

Since there are no "others," and all are aspects of oneself, when we say we take in the suffering of others and give back joy, this is all taking place within us. You are responsible for everyone. The other who is suffering is yourself. That is why Master Jesus said, "Do unto others as you would have them do unto you," for the other is you. This idea of oneness was beautifully expressed by the 16th century English poet, John Donne:

Send not to know for whom the bell tolls,

It tolls for thee.

Giving and Receiving *(tonglen)* begins with *shamatha*, observing your inbreath and outbreath. When you are calm and centered in the sensitive area in the center of your chest that we call the heart (actually beneath the sternum), think of someone or some group of people experiencing suffering. It could be a friend or someone you read about in the news. Imagine what they are experiencing, physically, mentally, emotionally, and spiritually. Imagine you are there with them, that you are them. You feel what they are feeling, think what they are thinking. It is very basic. Even if you are in the desert or in the mountains, you are connected with others through the etheric web.

As you exhale you feel love going out to them on your breath like rays of light from the sun in your heart. As these rays enter their hearts, you bring them solace, freedom from suffering, peace, and freedom. As you inhale, you sense the suffering; as you exhale you see the darkness within and around them dispersing and dissolving into light. In reality, there is no giving and receiving for their suffering is your suffering and your enlightenment is their enlightenment. Realizing that what affects you affects all, grounds you in the reality of your purpose, who you are, and where you are going.

Caution: Do not try to actually take on the suffering of others, for that can lead to taking on a condition you may not be able to transmute. This contradicts how tonglen is taught in some schools of thought.

Tibetan lamas imprisoned by the Chinese Communists told me that this method of seeing the "enemy" as an aspect of yourself that needs to be transmuted, saved them from despair and protected them from deeper psychological trauma. They felt the cruelty of the guards, but instead of reacting with anger they saw it as ignorance and sent love in return. Thus, many of these lamas were able to avoid Post Traumatic Stress Disorder (PTSD).

This is no different than what Jesus taught,[9]

> *Love your enemies.*
>
> *Do good to those who hate you.*
>
> *Bless those who curse you.*
>
> *Pray for those who mistreat you.*

-Luke 6:27-29

---

[9] There is considerable evidence in India that Jesus (known in ancient times as Issa) studied Buddhism and was a guest speaker at the Fourth Buddhist Council in Srinagar, Kashmir around CE 127-151.

Basic Goodness

The essence of God is a living spark of Light that is in everyone. That spark is what causes your heart to beat, your lungs to breathe, and every system in your body to function. Every second that spark, your I AM Presence, transmits signals to continue your life. Those sparks originate from the same Source that is within everyone, even those who do bad things. The spark comes from God and will return to God, so someday they too will return to the embrace of their True Self.

If you judge another or think limiting thoughts about another, you put an obstacle on their path of self-realization—and also place a block in your own path. Being aware of the Inner Light, the basic goodness in everyone, changes how you relate to people. This goodness is not only in people, but in every animal, blade of grass, and sub-atomic particle. You can feel it.

This sacred flame is projected from the etheric realm of the I AM Presence downward through the top of the head to a focus near the thymus gland below the sternum. You can feel it. This sensation is what people mean when they say, "I feel it in my heart." It is not the physical heart but a subtle feeling in the center of your chest. In India it is called the *Jyoti,* divine light, or what Trungpa Rinpoche called, "the soft spot."

Forgiveness

The Violet Tara is the Goddess of Forgiveness, as it is the Violet Flame that dissolves injuries and discord and raises us into a higher frequency. Only through forgiveness can this freedom be achieved; otherwise you come back lifetime after lifetime to work out your unresolved issues. The above practice of giving and receiving leads naturally to forgiveness, for the first step to healing is forgiveness. You may judge actions, but not the people acting, for everyone has basic goodness. See everyone as your child whom you will love even if they do something wrong. That is how the Masters see us. Where would we be if the Masters got angry at us every time we did something selfish or stupid?

If you want to heal others, you must do more than let go of the thought of blame, but actually release the emotional charge you have regarding them. Perhaps while doing the previous practice of sending and receiving you had the thought that the reason those people were suffering was because they did something wrong. That may be, but it may also be because of something you did wrong toward them in a past life. You don't know all you did in past lives that may have contributed to their condition. Since you don't know everything, change the judgment of others to:

I am responsible for all those who are

actually aspects of myself.

If you judge those who suffer, you ensure that someday you will have that same experience. This is an inexorable process by which we trade roles life after life until we forgive each other for everything. The prostitute becomes a nun, and the nun who feels superior becomes a prostitute, finally arriving at innate purity. Likewise, the criminal and policeman change roles, finally developing over many lifetimes an understanding of the law and respect for others. Remember the well-known Native American saying,

Do not judge another until you have walked

for two moons in their moccasins.

-Cherokee Tribe

Ask the Violet Tara for her assistance in letting go of old judgments and their energies that may be embedded, not only in the hidden recesses of your mind, but in the very cells of your body. Ask her to help dissolve all cause, effect, memory and record of any past hurtful deeds. It is those memories stored in the subconscious that need to be dissolved and consumed by the Violet Fire. This requires the following:

1) **Understand** the causes that led others to their actions.

2) **Accept** that they acted out of ignorance or limited understanding.

3) **Do not punish** others, for everyone receives back what they have sent out.

4) See the **basic goodness** in everyone.
5) **Let go,** and rest in non-judgmental awareness, free of all concepts.

Also, think of the word "forgive" as "I give you before:"

> I gave you the opportunity to do what you
> did as this may have been a lesson you could
> not learn any other way. I, too, have hurt
> others, and am grateful for those experiences
> from which I have learned.
> I am forgiven for what I did wrong,
> so I pray to Almighty God to forgive you
> as I have been forgiven.

As Jesus said:

> *If we say that we have no sin,*
> *we deceive ourselves....*

-1 John 1:8

Still the Mind with Six Nails

On the most basic level all spiritual practice begins with slowing the mind, for only when compulsive thought processes slow can we truly perceive reality. This can be difficult as the mind is always alert and on guard for any possible threat; and the mind creates the ego to judge how well it is doing. To begin a spiritual practice without first stilling the mind is like trying to light a candle in a hurricane. Here is a practice to still the mind given by the Indian sage, Tilopa, called The Six Nails[10]:

1) **Let go of the past.**
2) **Let go of the future.**
3) **Let go of what is happening now.**
4) **Don't try to figure anything out.**

---

[10] Tilopa was the 11th century Bengali mahasiddha who was born to a royal family and became a wandering monk. One day the Goddess Matangi appeared and told him that in order to achieve enlightenment he needed to let go of his judgments and become a pimp for a prostitute. During the day he ran a mill crushing sesame seeds, hence his name derived from the Sanskrit *til* for sesame seed. Working at these two jobs, he achieved enlightenment and acquired extraordinary powers. He became the teacher of Naropa, the teacher of Marpa, who became the guru of Milarepa, thus beginning the Kagyu lineage of Buddhism. One of his famous remarks was, "The problem is not enjoyment, but attachment to enjoyment."

5) **Don't try to make anything happen.**
6) **Relax, right now, and awake!**

This meditation advice could be summed up in the words of Bhagavan Das. He brought Ram Dass, the former Harvard professor who influenced a generation of American youth, to Neem Karoli Baba:[11]

Be here now!

The previous *shamatha* and *vipassana* instructions lead to this awareness of the present moment—equivalent to clearing the ground before constructing a temple. You do not build on rough ground or a site overgrown with brush and weeds, but on smooth ground with a spacious view. Now that your mind is still and you are totally present, go to the next section where you will invite Violet Tara to reside in the temple of your awareness.

---

[11] *Be Here Now!* (Lama Foundation, 1978).

Invoking God

What image of God is most real to you? Many Westerners grew up seeing God as depicted by Michelangelo on the ceiling of the Sistine Chapel, an old man with a white beard sitting on a cloud. Some grew up believing in Santa Claus, an omniscient deity-like being who rewards good actions.[12] In India there are thousands of Gods, all understood to be aspects of the one formless God, Para Brahman, and who are invoked for every conceivable purpose. Each one becomes real to the extent of your devotion and

---

[12] Santa Claus evolved over the past thousand years or so as a combination of the Turkish Saint Nicolaus who gave to the poor and the British, Father Christmas, who encouraged revelry. Both versions were slender and did not give presents. Not until 19th century England was he connected with the giving of presents. In 1837 An American poet Clement Clark wrote the poem, "Twas the night before Christmas". The flying reindeer of the poem come from a shamanic vision had by Siberian nomads dating back 3,000 years. The vision came from consuming the Amanita muscaria mushroom which they saw the deer eating. All these traditions were united by Coca Cola, Inc. in 1931 to create a corpulent Santa who drank Coke and gave children presents. Walt Disney later enhanced the image. At one time he was depicted as carrying a black birch rod to punish naughty children, and his robe has varied in color from brown, to green, blue, and finally red.

focused energy. These Gods have been created by the focused collective attention of millions of people visualizing and praying to them over thousands of years. They are not empty images but are real according to the individual's acceptance of and focus upon them—since what your attention is upon you bring into being.[13] Hence you create Gods in your own image—until you find the Source that is the ultimate Creator.

---

[13] During the Harmonic Convergence, a New Age phenomenon that occurred in 1987, a crowd gathered in Mount Shasta to see an image that appeared on a woman's TV screen. Many "psychics" channeled messages from the being, variously described as an Angel, the Spirit of the Convergence, a commander of a space ship, and Sananda (a name for Jesus channeled by Sister Thedra). I saw a mother hold her infant against the TV screen for a blessing. When a TV repair man showed up and said, "Lady, you've got a bad capacitor; do you want me to fix it?" she replied, "No, that would be sacrilege." To this day, she is convinced an angel had appeared in her home and remains uplifted by the belief.

The idea which man calls "God" only exists in the consciousness of man himself. We do not resemble Him, He resembles us.

-Sir Edward Bulwer-Lytton (1803-1873, author of *Zanoni*, inspired by Saint Germain)

Today, many New Age Gods, Masters, and beings from other dimensions are being created and "channeled" by those with good imaginations. As people come to believe in these beings and their messages, these entities attain greater reality and people become dependent on them for ever more information. This is not only unnecessary, but dangerous. As you learn to still the mind and contact your Source, the need for intermediaries and their fabricated messages disappears. Only self-knowledge leads to empowerment and Mastery. The difference between the practice of tantra, in which a deity is created and dissolved in meditation, and the New Age practice in which beings are created to give messages, is that the tantric practitioner knows these deities are self-created—and ultimately dissolves them into primordial awareness along with ego-clinging. This lessens the individual's tendency toward self-cherishing, while channeling leads to the enhancement of ego through the feeling that one is so special as to merit receipt of a message from a superior being.

The way to self-mastery through the creation and dissolution of a meditational deity is given here in the tantric practice of the Violet Tara. Tantra[14] is an advanced practice first requiring completion of certain preliminaries that help you realize the nature of mind. Without practicing these preliminaries there is the danger you think you permanently become the Deity and cherish this illusory self rather than seeing that the same Deity is in everyone. If done correctly, you will realize through this practice that *nothing is real* except Consciousness. Then you will have compassion and your greatest desire will be to help others achieve freedom from suffering. To avoid the pitfall of self-cherishing the human ego, it is important to start at the beginning. Purify the mind-stream and arrive at the realization of basic goodness and humility.

---

[14]Tantra is also known as *Vajrayana* (Sanskrit: vehicle of sudden, indestructible realization).

"I Am" is the Key

The key to all creation is in the expression, "I Am," said in whatever language is closest to your heart. In Sanskrit it is *Soham*. The previous practices have been given to subdue the ego and prepare the mind for the use of this key to open the doors of Creation. In this way, "I" does not refer to the ego, which is impermanent. Meditate on the source of "I" and you will achieve God Consciousness. Say "I Am" and you bring that Consciousness into manifestation. "I" is self-referent to the God you are. Observe how many times throughout the day you say or think "I." What do you connect with "I," and is that what you want? The practices given here will help you be more conscious of what you create. Ultimately, you can create a new world.

The Preliminaries

To everything there is a beginning, middle, and end. The same goes for the attainment of enlightenment and the accomplishments (Sanskrit: *siddhas)* of Mastery. After first taking refuge in the **Three Jewels:** the Buddha, Dharma and Sangha, you begin a series of practices called *ngondro,* the preliminaries.

The **Initial Preliminaries** consist of meditating on the **Four Thoughts:**

1) **Preciousness of life**—gratitude to be alive.
2) **Impermanence**—your life could end any moment.
3) **Karma**—your present circumstances were created by your past actions.
4) **Samsara**—lasting happiness is not found in the ever-changing illusions of life.

The **Secondary Preliminaries,** which begins the tantric training, consists of four practices. (All tantric practice employs mantra, mudra (physical gesture or action), and visualization, which are further discussed later):

1) Commitment to the **Teacher** (lama, guru).
2) Commitment to the **Deity** (*yiddam,* meditational beings that you generate and later dissolve).
3) Commitment to the **Ascended Master** (*dakini/daka)* guiding you.
4) Commitment to do **prostrations** (a traditional practice that stabilizes your commitment and

generates humility and compassion. Traditionally you do 100,000 full body prostrations during which you visualize the **I AM Presence** before you (traditionally Vajrasattva, the source of all Deities). However, as most people don't have the time to take a year to do these, I suggest you do at least one full body prostrations daily to the I AM Presence in front of and slightly above you, surrounded by rainbow light. The Presence is surrounded by the Ascended Masters of the Seven Rays, Great Divine Director, Quan Yin, Maitreya, Jesus, Mother Mary, and others of the Ascended Council of Light.[15] Also, visualize in front of you all enemies or those you feel you have

---

[15] I am using the term, Council of Light in place of Great White Brotherhood, as this spiritual organization that exists on the etheric plane is composed of female as well as male Masters that originate from different races with different skin colors. However, "white" pertains here to the color of their robes or the white light they emanate). Nor do they think of themselves as "great." Theosophy calls them Elder Brothers or Adepts. "Ascended Master," is a recent term. Previously they have been called arisen ones, bodhisattvas, devas, and *dakas* and *dakinis* (Sanskrit: sky dancer, both male and female). *Mahasiddha* (Sanskrit) generally applies to a masterful being still in physical form, who may have the power to appear in multiple places simultaneously, precipitate objects, and have many other powers.

negative karma with—those who have opposed or harmed you. Since they are ultimately inseparable from you, pray that this practice benefits them also. Visualize beside and behind you: your parents, family, friends, associates, and sangha, who prostrate with you. This prostration may also be done internally if practiced with sincere devotion.

While prostrating, recite this prayer:

Commitment to the I AM Presence

From now until I ascend,

I commit myself to the I AM Presence,

to spiritual practice, and to the Ascended

Masters of the Council of Light.

Each prostration is done by first raising your palms together in prayer above your head. The clasped hands are then brought down consecutively to your brow, throat, and heart—representing enlightened body, speech, and mind. Then stoop down with your knees on the ground, hands in front and to the side of your knees. Slide forward, stretching full length on the ground, stretching your arms and hands straight forward. Your forehead touches the ground. While prostrate, clasp your hands together in prayer and then bring them back above your head. Then place your hands on the ground, using them to push yourself to standing position. Clasp your hands in prayer over your heart and begin again. As you rise from the prostration, recite this prayer:

Until all beings are liberated,

I will bring about benefit and happiness

For all beings who have been my mothers.

Since time is an illusion and we live in eternity, everyone has been or eventually will be your mother. Hence, we need to show kindness to all. Tradition requires that the 100,000 prostrations be completed before beginning tantric practice; however, it is not just the physical action that is important, but the sincerity and consciousness with which the prostrations are done. Thus, it is conceivable that a parent could realize the same benefit by taking care of their child if done with sincere intent. See the child as an embodiment of God, see parenthood as a spiritual practice, and see the child as a future member of the Council of Light. Dedicate the raising of the child to the benefit of humanity.

Taking care of anyone, if done with the right motivation, will develop the same humility and compassion as prostrating. While I was in Tibet, I was deeply moved to see people walking across vast plains doing full body prostrations every third step on their way to Lhasa. Some were old and it was a pilgrimage that took months—an act of true surrender and dedication.

Prayer to the I AM Presence:

Traditionally a Sanskrit prayer to Vajrasattva, the God of Purity who can also be seen as the origin of all other Gods, would be recited here; however, I suggest praying to I AM Presence, which also embodies those same qualities and is the origin of yourself:

O Beloved I AM Presence, protect my commitment to you and remain committed to me. Increase all that is positive and good within me. Be loving towards me and grant success. Show me the consequences of all actions before I act. Make my mind good, virtuous, and auspicious! May I attain your essence of happiness and achieve full realization in all my bodies. Grant me all empowerments and joys of realization. Ah! Blessed One who is the embodiment of all the Masters, do not abandon me. Help me realize my

own indestructible nature and make me one with you.[16]

Mandala Offering: Next offer up everything that you consider yours to your I AM Presence for the benefit of all beings. Mandala is the Sanskrit word for circle, but here it is the universe. Since the essence of tantra is to see the oneness of the outer and inner realities, to affect real change you need physical, symbolic objects to make the offering complete.

Place a cloth before you to hold the various ritual objects: rice to represent nourishment; precious or semiprecious gems, jewelry, and coins, to represent wealth; and any other objects representing things of value to which you may feel attached. Place a ball or picture of the Earth on the cloth also. You may also place a picture of the I AM Presence or whichever Master you feel closest to on the far side of the cloth. This is your mandala. Now, pick up a handful of the grains, gems, and other objects in your hand and pour them over the ball or picture, and offer them up for the benefit of all sentient beings.

Say this prayer:

---

[16] This is an approximate translation from the Sanskrit of the Vajrasattva mantra, also known as the 100-Syllable Mantra.

Mandala Prayer

I offer all the bodies, wealth, splendor, and attainments that I have ever had or will ever attain in this and all future lifetimes, for the benefit of all sentient beings.

This practice releases all attachments, egotism, and self-cherishing if done with a pure heart. Done correctly with inner focus, what you visualize and dedicate inwardly manifests throughout all levels of your being. Traditionally, this preliminary practice is also completed 100,000 times before aspiring to the next level of Deity Creation.

Guru Yoga, (meaning to merge with the Guru) is the next step. This visualization helps further purify the mind of egoic delusion so that its true nature is revealed as one with the Guru, which is ultimately your I AM Presence. The Universal Guru is a manifestation of God, your True Self. In other words, God, Guru, and Self are One. In Tibet this is accompanied by the recitation of the Seven Line Prayer to Guru Rinpoche (Padmasambhava), who introduced Vajrayana Buddhism to southern Tibet; however, since the Master Saint Germain is the initiator of this practice now in the West, pray to him. Visualize or place a picture of him before you as you pray:

Seven Line Prayer to Saint Germain[17]

Beloved Saint Germain,

you who are guiding humanity

to knowledge of their own Divinity,

I ask your blessings on my efforts

to attain full enlightenment and mastery,

so I may work for the liberation of all

beings. I know That I AM One with you!

As you still your mind, eyes partially closed, imagine that the actual, living, breathing Master has heard you and materialized for your benefit. In reality, whenever you think of Saint Germain or say his name, he is aware of your attention. Gradually, see him become more and more luminous until he becomes a sun of violet light that merges with you. Then affirm and feel:

I am the presence of Saint Germain,

Master of the Violet Consuming Flame.

---

[17] Traditionally, Tibetans chant a seven line prayer to Guru Rinpoche (Padmasambhava), but Saint Germain is better known in the West. However, you would also derive great benefit from the Guru Rinpoche mantra: *Om Ah Hung Vajra Guru Padma Siddhi Hung.*

Repeat this affirmation 108 times, then gradually dissolve the visualization. Observe the space on the floor before you and feel your inbreath and outbreath. Return to empty, non-conceptual awareness, and be at peace.

Archangel Michael

Lastly, invoke **Archangel Michael.** His action is more intense and sudden than that of Saint Germain, so invoke the Violet Flame first to begin the purification process. Visualize him in front of and above you and see yourself becoming one with him. Archangel Michael will clear all ego-clinging, attachments, ignorance, false concepts, negative energy, or any other obstacle on your path to enlightenment. He appears in shining armor and wields a sword of blue flame, commanding the Legions of Angels of the Blue Lightning of Divine Love. Visualize, invoke, and call them into action to free all people, places, conditions, and things from any negative condition or limitation whatsoever:

I am the presence of Archangel Michael wielding the Sword of Blue Flame, blazing forth to cut all free from all limitation whatsoever.

I am the Presence of the Angels of the Blue Lightning of Divine Love, charging forth wherever needed, freeing humanity this very moment from all negativity, illusion, ignorance, or any other limitation whatsoever, by the Power of God

That I Am!

Gradually dissolve the visualization. Observe the space on the floor before you and feel your inbreath and outbreath. Return to empty, non-conceptual awareness, and be at peace.

Kama Tantra[18]

The most challenging aspect of duality is that of the female and male polarity. Perhaps it is so challenging because those are aspects of reality all the way up to the final merging in the Absolute. It is that dichotomy of energy that holds the electron in its orbit around the nucleus of the atom. It permeates all aspects of nature from the microbe to the very relationship between matter and anti-matter.

Yogic science recognizes these dual energies as one of the prime motivating drives of human existence, and so seeks to channel that awareness inward toward God-realization, rather than outward into romance and reproduction.

One of the ancient Tibetan books dealing with this is the *Six Yogas of Naropa,* a little read and even lesser understood text. The first part discusses the use of that dual energy to kindle the inner heat, a practice known in Tibetan as *tuomo*. It is by this practice that yogis can spend winters in caves in snow-bound mountains wearing only thin cotton garments. Achieving the basic understanding of this method requires approximately three years. Then one can go on to the other methods of evolution, awakening, and self-mastery. One of the final

---

[18] In some texts this is called *karma* yoga; however, this translates from Sanskrit as the yoga of selfless action, so well described in the *Bhagavad Gita.* Since *kama* translates from the Sanskrit as desire, I will continue to call this practice of transmuting desire: kama yoga, not karma yoga.

practices teaches the science of the union of the male and female bio-electric currents. This is not about having better sex, but about transcending sexual desire entirely.

In fact, only the least evolved yogi needs to practice with another human being. The more advanced yogis practice with increasingly subtle emanations of duality. That could involve practicing consciously with another person whose physical form is at a distance; practicing with a visualized Deity; and finally, the practice of uniting the two currents within oneself directly. All forms of the practice eventually lead to this inner union.

To begin the spiritual practice the male is visualized sitting in lotus position, legs crossed, and spine upright. The female is visualized sitting in the male's lap, legs wrapped around his torso, arms wrapped around him. The man's arms wrap around the woman's form. The figures kiss, with tongues joined in each other's mouths. They are joined together in sexual union; however, instead of releasing the energy in orgasm, the flow is directed as a flame that blazes upward through the central channel and energizing the chakras until one attains enlightenment. The male and female energies merge in *satchitananda:* being, consciousness, and bliss.

This final part is accomplished by imagining the merging of the subtle nervous systems, the male and female subtle channels joining together, one's tongue against the roof of one's mouth. In this way the gross physical aspect dissolves in the union of the two energy systems, whose natural impetus is to raise upward through the central channel within the spine. One visualizes oneself seated in a giant lotus blossom floating in a sea of consciousness. Underneath one, within the rectum, is a sapphire blazing with blue light. Some of this blue light goes straight down, joining with a great, blazing blue light in the center of the earth.

As the breath is drawn in, it is inhaled up the central channel, drawing the conscious life force with it, conducting it up to the solar plexus chakra, heart chakra, throat chakra, brow chakra, and finally crown chakra at the top of the head. One can imaging these chakras as lotus flowers blooming as the life force enters and passes up through them. As the energy reaches the crown chakra, it joins with the light coming down from the Higher Self, the *atman* (Tibetan: *dharmakaya*). Thus, the brow chakra is also illuminated. As the breath is further exhaled, so is the light with it, descending the front part of the central channel through the tongue, and thence to the heart.

Eventually, the lower three chakras, which are reflections of the upper three chakras, dissolve into their higher aspects. Then you become a sphere of light, the masculine and feminine having merged in the God Conscious dharmakaya, the I AM Presence.

Invocation of the Violet Tara

One of the main accomplishments of this practice is the understanding and ultimate attainment of the Deity within yourself.[19] This Deity was not a historical person who lived on Earth, not an Angel, nor Ascended Master, but a Deity you call forth from your own Consciousness who reveals to you an aspect of yourself. It begins as what esotericism would call a thought-form but created in the image of a God. However, your practice takes it beyond that. By mastering this practice, you can be in multiple places and frequencies simultaneously, as well as master the physical plane. The purpose is not to replace the Masters, but to help you tap in to the same Source as the Masters. You need to learn how to do what the Masters do rather than rely on them for everything—for it is only in practicing mastery that you become a Master. Creating a Deity is an act of your own God Power, for you are a Creator, an embodiment of self-existing, innate unlimited consciousness. This enables you to be whatever you wish, to recreate yourself in whatever form and with whatever attributes you desire.

Now you will invoke and become the Violet Tara. She manifests the aspect of the Divine Mother that dissolves ignorance, judgments, negative energy, and raises everything her gaze rests upon into a state of higher purity and perfection. Her consciousness is present everywhere

---

[19] In Vajrayana practice this Deity would be known as a *yiddam,* a manifestation of consciousness you create in meditation to realize as an aspect of yourself.

and at all times just as violet light is always present in white light—so she is present in our consciousness, waiting to be invoked. You don't see violet light until white light passes through a prism or raindrops and is diffracted into its constituent colors. As the Divine Mother has given birth to everything in nature, the violet light is one of her expressions as much as the flowers of the Earth.

Saint Germain, as the Chohan (head) of the 7th Ray, helps direct this activity on the Earth for the benefit of humanity. It is through his initiative that the Council of Light has allowed him to teach this activity to his students. He now enlists our support to manifest this purifying activity. Even without following the steps given here, you can always invoke the Violet Consuming Flame by your own sincere thoughts and actions. Simply by meditating, the purifying activity of the Violet Flame takes place to some degree on its own. However, the practices given here amplify its activity to a much greater degree.

Deity creation begins the same way all creation takes place—with a vision. Then comes verbal enunciation of what you desire (through affirmation or mantra)—then comes acceptance.

Visualize what you want. An artist starts with an image in mind; a carpenter who wants to make a chair starts with the thought of a chair. Here, you will focus on the thought and image of **Violet Tara**.

First, dedicate your anticipated action for the benefit of humanity.[20] Enter a state of peaceful awareness, free of thoughts, allowing your mind to settle in the soft spot near your heart. See yourself seated in a beautiful amethyst temple with amethyst pillars and a floor of white marble. Outside the temple stand the Lords of the Four Directions. In the sky surrounding the temple are the Seven Mighty Elohim (Hebrew: Gods). These are manifestations of the seven spirits (Sanskrit: *Saptarishis*) that emanated from the Source, whose activity is carried out on Earth by the seven Elohim, the seven Ascended Masters, Saint Germain being the Elohim of the Seventh Ray.

Standing before you is Violet Tara, made of violet light, offering in her hands an amethyst, sword, and mala. These represent the three aspects of all tantric practice: mantra, mudra, and visualization. Her arms are outstretched toward you, and myriad rays of violet light emanate from her heart to yours. Pray as follows to Saint Germain for this vision to be empowered.

---

[20] There is an ancient tantric practice to achieve ego lessness in which the body and all thoughts of self are offered as food to the Gods.

Request for Empowerment

Beloved Master Saint Germain, please
Empower this Deity and make her real.
Manifest the Violet Tara in my life
Right now, fully self-sustained,
A living Goddess
For the benefit of all!

Then Invoke the Goddess Tara, who is now present and fully aware of you:

Invocation

O Great Violet Tara,
Beloved Divine Mother,
You who are an emanation
Of the Light from the Heart of Creation
With which I am One,
I implore you,
Release your Violet Fire of Purification
through my mind, feelings, and world.

Purify and transmute wherever needed this
Very moment!
Thank you!
I know it is already done!

Become Violet Tara

Meditate on and visualize yourself as Violet Tara, repeating inwardly:

I am Violet Tara!

Repeat her *mantra* (Sanskrit: mind protection) 108 times with great love, feeling her energy blaze up, around, and through you:

I am Tara of Violet Fire,

I am the Purity God Desires!

To transmit Her Blessings, while still manifesting yourself as Violet Tara, repeat:

I am Violet Tara, Radiant Goddess from

the Heart of Creation. I am pouring forth

love, purity, wisdom, and forgiveness

wherever needed—transmuting everything

into its inherent perfection and bringing

God's Divine Plan to Earth

this very moment!

So be it!

Maintain simultaneously your focus on the Flame in the center of your chest and also the Goddess before you. Feel the rays of Violet Light radiate from her heart to yours. More and more love pours forth from her to you. She forgives you unconditionally and feels your love and gratitude to her. Her love becomes more and more intense until she dissolves completely in Violet Light. She merges with your own heart, mind, body, and soul. Now you are the Violet Tara. Rays of violet light pour forth from your third eye, your heart, and the palms of your hands—radiating in all directions—throughout all dimensions and universes. You are now the Goddess at the Center of Creation. Your grace, forgiveness, and purification raise all into their innate Perfection. Use your power now to dissolve and consume all imperfection, ignorance, and suffering immediately.

Dissolution

Gradually dissolve your Goddess aspect and return to non-conceptual self-awareness. Eyes open, observe the space before you. Sit in non-conceptual awareness, knowing that all others are also yourself. You are calm and peaceful, filled with the Nectar of the Goddess. Her energy is within you, radiating through you to bless others wherever you go.

As an option, you may take this realization a step further at the conclusion of the practice by asking the Violet Tara to reside above you. Visualize her seated on a moon disk resting on a sun disk inside a lotus blossom on above your head. Ask her to bless everyone you encounter or think about. Ask her, "Beloved Goddess, during the day, please act on your own wherever needed."

People will feel her blessings and wonder what happened to them. Strengthen this activity by saying her mantra or by saying silently:

I AM Violet Tara in action here now!

She will then manifest and radiate the Violet Consuming Flame, dissolve and consume disharmony, and radiate love without any effort on your part. In the same way you can also invoke Saint Germain, who is your elder brother, and who is doing the same work with the Violet Flame on many planes of existence. He will be grateful for your help for he is very busy. Done regularly and with devotion, this practice will purify and raise, not only you, but all humanity.

Gratitude

We give thanks, O Tara,

For your grace, guidance, and blessings.

Please help us remember you.

Be with us always!

We thank you.

Note

These practices are powerful aids to enlightenment and liberation if done correctly. Their most fundamental purpose is to train the mind, subdue ego, and generate compassion. If you feel those qualities increasing, then you know you are practicing correctly. If they seem too complicated, you can do as Jesus suggested to his disciples when they asked him to simplify his teachings. He reduced his message to these two commands:

Love God with all your heart,

soul, and mind.

Love your neighbor as yourself.

If that is too difficult, simply try to help others.

The Nature of Mind

Since pure awareness of nowness is the real Buddha, in openness and contentment I found the Lama in my heart. When we realize this unending natural mind is the very nature of the Lama, then there is no need for attached, grasping, or weeping prayers or artificial complaints. By simply relaxing in this uncontrived, open, and natural state, we obtain the blessing of aimless self-liberation of whatever arises.

No words can describe it,

No example can point to it,

Samsara does not make it worse,

Nirvana does not make it better,

It has never been born,

It has never ceased,

It has never been liberated,

It has never been deluded,

It has never existed,

It has never been nonexistent,

It has no limits at all,

It does not fall into any kind of category.

-Dudjom Rinpoche

Peter Mt. Shasta and his guide, Yongdu, Samye Monastery, Tibet, 1997

www.ingramcontent.com/pod-product-compliance
Lightning Source LLC
Chambersburg PA
CBHW050442010526
44118CB00013B/1638